WORLD OF SPORTS

SCUBA DIVING

Published by Smart Apple Media
123 South Broad Street, Mankato, Minnesota 56001

Photography: pages 7, 9, 10, 11, 15, 30—CORBIS/Stephen
Frink; page 14—CORBIS/Bettmann;
page 16—CORBIS/Lawson Wood; page 22—CORBIS/Rick
Price; page 29—CORBIS/Amos Nachoum

Design and Production by EvansDay Design

LIBRARY OF CONGRESS CATALOGING-IN-PUBLICATION DATA

Vander Hook, Sue, 1949–
Scuba diving / by Sue Vander Hook.
p. cm. — (World of sports)
Includes index.
Summary: Surveys the history, equipment, techniques,
risks, and safety factors of scuba diving.
ISBN 1-887068-59-7
1. Scuba diving—Juvenile literature. [1. Scuba diving.]
I. Title. II. Series: World of sports (Mankato, Minn.)
GV838.672.V36   2000
797.2'3—dc21   98-36410

9 8 7 6 5 4 3 2

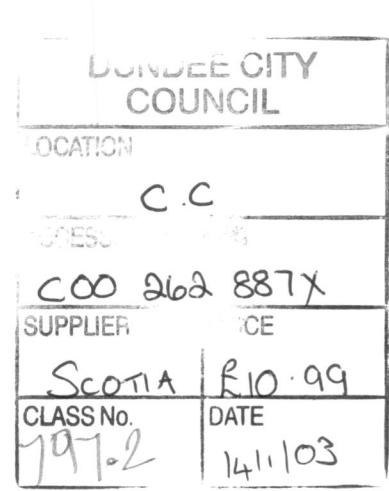

SCUBA DIVING

SUE VANDER HOOK

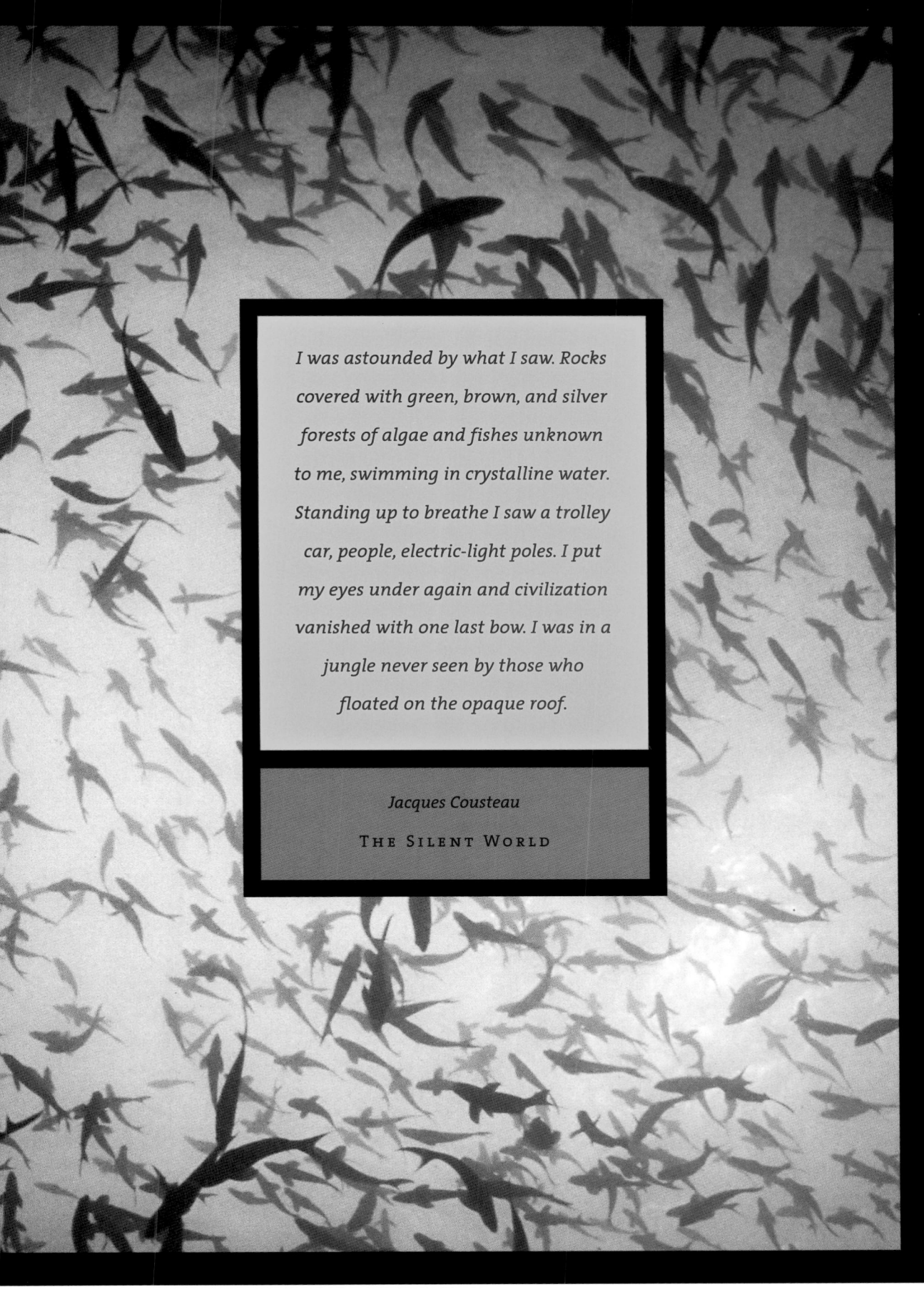

I was astounded by what I saw. Rocks covered with green, brown, and silver forests of algae and fishes unknown to me, swimming in crystalline water. Standing up to breathe I saw a trolley car, people, electric-light poles. I put my eyes under again and civilization vanished with one last bow. I was in a jungle never seen by those who floated on the opaque roof.

Jacques Cousteau

THE SILENT WORLD

Underwater Exploration

THE UNDERWATER WORLD can be a dangerous place, one that lacks air and has pressure strong enough to crush human bodies. Nevertheless, diving with the proper training and equipment is a safe, thrilling way to explore the natural beauty and boundless treasures of the aquatic realm. After a person obtains scuba diving certification, three-fourths of the world becomes a new frontier to explore. Accompanied by a second certified diver, a scuba diver can venture into almost any body of water on Earth.

A bathyscaphe set a world record in 1960 for the deepest dive. Jacques Piccard and navy lieutenant Donald Walsh descended 35,800 feet (10,912 m) into the **Marianas Trench** *of the Pacific Ocean.*

Many people dive simply to enjoy the pristine beauty of the sea. Although humans are strangers in the aquatic world, most species that live there seem undisturbed by the presence of people. In fact, fish that carefully avoid taking a baited hook will often eat food from a diver's hand. Many fish seem curious about human intruders and swim around divers as if they want to play. Divers are likely to see a rainbow

of fish varieties and even dolphins and whales in certain regions of the sea. No other sport in the world gives people the opportunity to play tag with seals or sea lions.

For hundreds of years, people have been **free-diving** to explore the underwater world. Divers have gathered oysters for their valuable pearls and shellfish for their expensive Tyrian purple dye. Japanese and Korean divers today still free-dive for oysters, shellfish, and sea-weed. Sponge divers were referred to in Homer's epic poem *Iliad*, a work that dates back to about 750 B.C. To stay underwater for longer periods of time, early divers began breathing through reeds with the tips just above the water's surface. Many divers today still use this diving technique by breathing through a **snorkel**.

Scuba divers called frogmen were used in Operation Desert Storm in 1991 to remove and defuse mines in Kuwaiti waters.

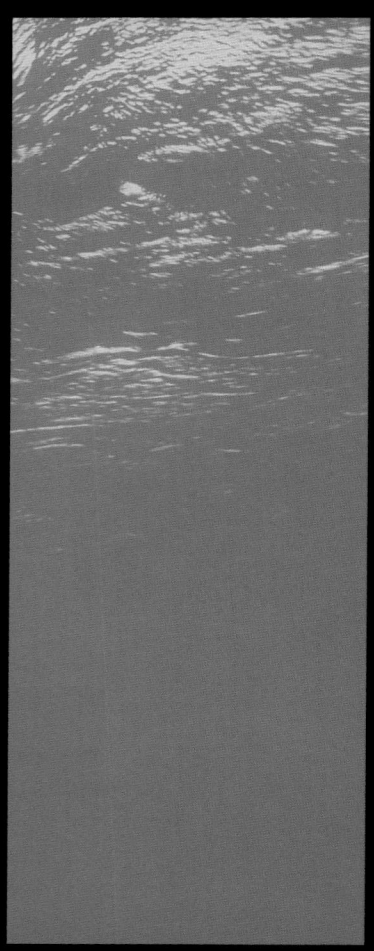

A WIDE ARRAY OF UN-
USUAL AND COLORFUL FISH
IS JUST ONE OF THE SPEC-
TACULAR SIGHTS TO BE
SEEN IN THE OCEAN.

A DIVER EXAMINES ENORMOUS
SPONGES GROWING ALONG A
CORAL REEF, A ROCKY LEDGE
FORMED BY FOSSILIZED SEA
LIFE REMAINS.

snorkel *a plastic or rubber mouthpiece shaped like a "J" through which a person breathes while swimming underwater close to the surface*

Over time, people have tried to make devices that would let them leave the surface of the water and observe the wonders of the deep. The first known diving equipment—from about 900 B.C.—consisted of an inflated animal bladder strapped to a diver's chest. In the fourth century B.C., the Macedonian ruler Alexander the Great was lowered into the ocean in a glass barrel that allowed him to see the underwater world. Other brave souls have attempted to descend in iron suits, diving cages, or other contraptions.

By 1680, Giovanni Borelli had designed a device operated by the diver using a hand pump for air supply. Thirty-six years later, Englishman Dr. Edmund Halley was sending barrels of fresh air down to divers in a diving bell made of

wood and bound with strips of metal. Divers could stay underwater for up to one and a half hours with this continuous air supply.

Jacques Cousteau's vessel, Calypso, *which had traveled the world's waters on research missions for 45 years, sank in port in murky Singapore waters after being hit by a barge. It was lifted out on January 26, 1996.*

The first major breakthrough in diving equipment came in 1819 when the Englishman Augustus Siebe invented the "hard hat." This metal helmet allowed the diver to receive air through an attached hose connected to an air pump on the surface. Though restricted in movement by heavy weights carried for **ballast**, the diver was free to explore under the sea for long periods of time. In 1837, Siebe invented a pressurized, insulated diving suit to be used with the helmet. This 900-

A DIVER EXAMINES AN UNUSUAL RING-SHAPED CORAL. DIVERS ARE OFTEN THE FIRST HUMANS EVER TO LAY EYES ON SUCH UNDERWATER STRUCTURES.

pound (409 kg) suit became the standard used by divers for more than a century.

By 1925, Commander Le Prieur of the French navy developed a tank filled with **compressed** air. Le Prieur's equipment had a mouthpiece and a hose attached to a regulator valve. By 1931, divers working on submarine rescues were receiving fresh air in pressurized air bottles sent down from the surface. Divers used similar breathing equipment in 1934 to recover the remains of the sunken ship *Lusitania*.

In the 1930s, four inventors were working on improvements to Siebe's heavy diving suit. They produced a "lung" in 1938 that freed the diver from the heavy weights. However, World War II interrupted its development.

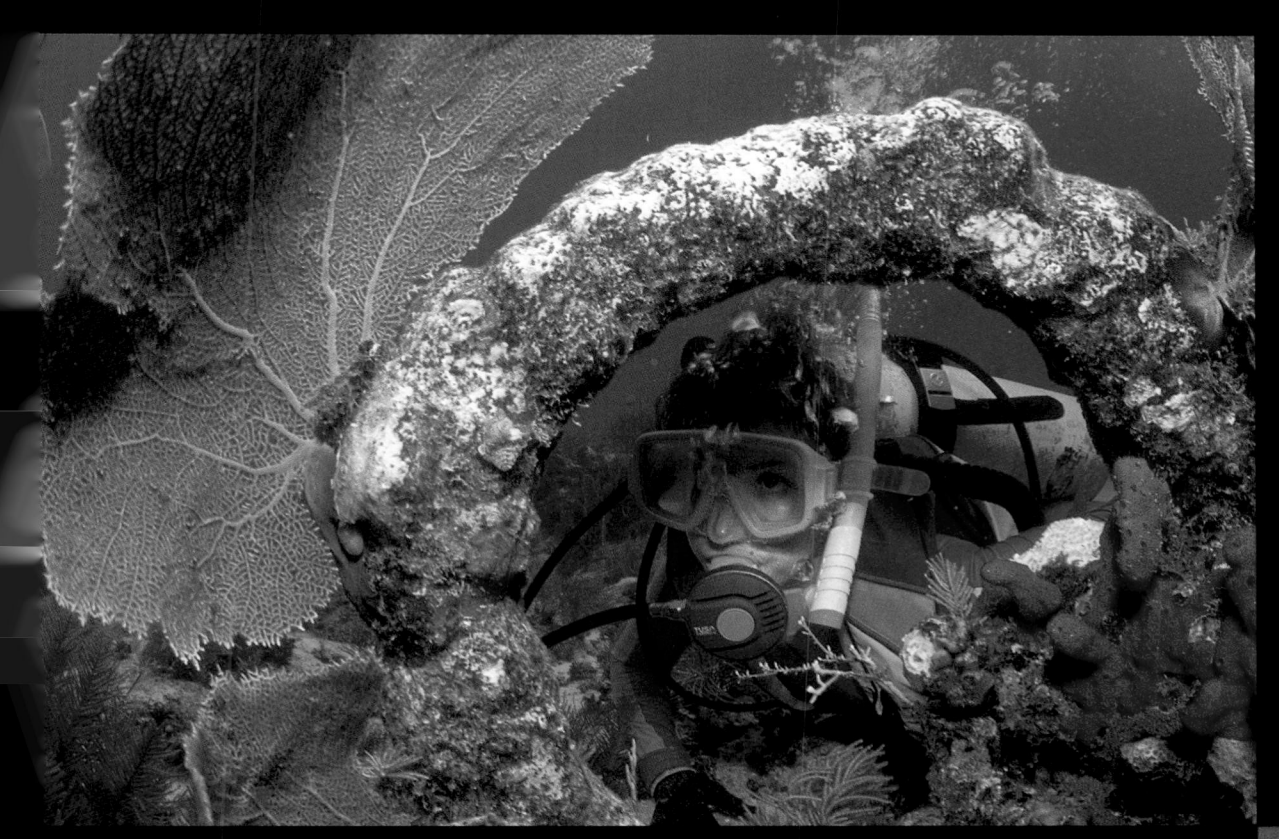

The Cousteau Legacy

AS RECENTLY AS 60 years ago, underwater divers had to rely on air that came from the surface. A long hose connected each diving suit to an air supply on a boat or on land. Divers wore canvas suits coated with rubber to protect them from the cold. Burdened by the heavy suits, weighted boots, and copper helmets, the divers moved slowly and carefully. Although they could see the underwater world, they couldn't go very far or very fast.

Today, divers can explore great depths without relying on surface equipment. Independence under the water was the result of one French navy officer's desire to make a significant contribution to the Allied forces during World War II. That officer was Jacques-Yves Cousteau.

During the war, the French were forced to sink their own ships to keep the Germans from seizing them. Cousteau devised a plan that

The first completely successful rescue of people trapped in a submarine took place in 1939. The McCann-Erickson Rescue Chamber took four trips down to 243 feet (74 m) to rescue 33 trapped men. The chamber fit over the submarine's escape hatch, allowing the men to enter the diving bell under one atmosphere of pressure.

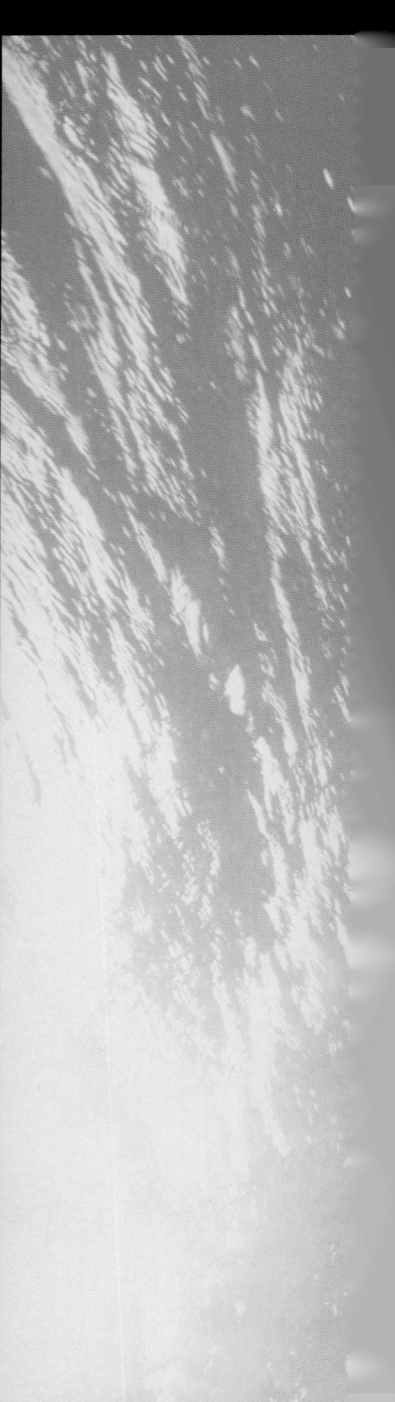

would let the French navy continue to fight the Germans. He wanted to equip navy divers with advanced, self-contained breathing equipment so they would not need hoses or surface air supplies. Divers could then spy on the Germans or plant underwater mines while avoiding enemy detection.

Cousteau had learned from British scientist John Scott Haldane that a diver's air supply had to be delivered at a pressure equal to that of the surrounding water. The Frenchman's greatest accomplishment was creating a breathing device that delivered compressed air at the proper pressure. Making an automatic regulating valve that responded to human breathing was the key to this achievement. In addition to giving air at the correct pressure to a diver at any depth, the valve also prevented dangerous

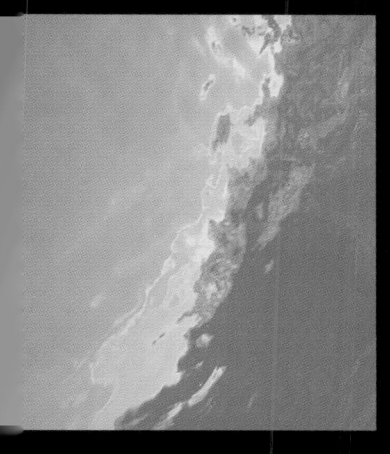

A SCUBA DIVER HOLDS ON TO A MECHANICAL PROPULSION DEVICE FOR GREATER SPEED WHILE SWIMMING.

amounts of carbon dioxide—released when the diver exhaled—from entering the tank.

In the spring of 1943, with the help of his father-in-law, Emile Gagnan, and a few close friends, Cousteau successfully created an air tank attached to a breathing device, an intake hose, an exhaust hose, and an air-flow regulator valve that would allow divers to swim independently. Even though the air tank weighed as much as 40 pounds (18 kg) on land, it felt nearly weightless in water. Cousteau obtained a **patent** for the device, which he called an Aqua Lung.

Unfortunately, Cousteau's invention came too late to help end the war. An Allied victory was already

The Duke University Medical chamber set a dive record in 1981, going to 2,250 feet (686 m). Stephen Porter, Len Whitlock, and Erik Kramer lived in the eight-foot-diameter (2.4 m) chamber for 43 days and beat their own record set the previous year.

underway. His vision of **frogmen** swimming freely underwater and attaching explosives to the hulls of enemy ships did not take place during World War II. However, the British military showed interest in Cousteau's Aqua Lung. They called it the Self-Contained Underwater Breathing Apparatus, although it is usually referred to by its acronym, SCUBA.

Shortly after World War II, the French navy employed a team of scuba divers led by Cousteau. The courageous divers defused thousands of underwater mines and bombs in depths down to 30 feet (9 m). They also removed live torpedoes from sunken German submarines.

Cousteau's group, called the Undersea Research Group, took great risks, but their work led to a legacy of underwater data. Group members spent the next several decades explor-

frogmen *swimmers equipped for lengthy underwater dives; in the military, divers may spy, plant explosives, or defuse mines*

coral reefs *hard, massive underwater structures formed by the skeletons of tiny sea animals*

JACQUES COUSTEAU AND HIS DIVING TEAM EXPLORE AND FILM THE WRECKAGE OF A RUSSIAN DESTROYER ON THE OCEAN FLOOR.

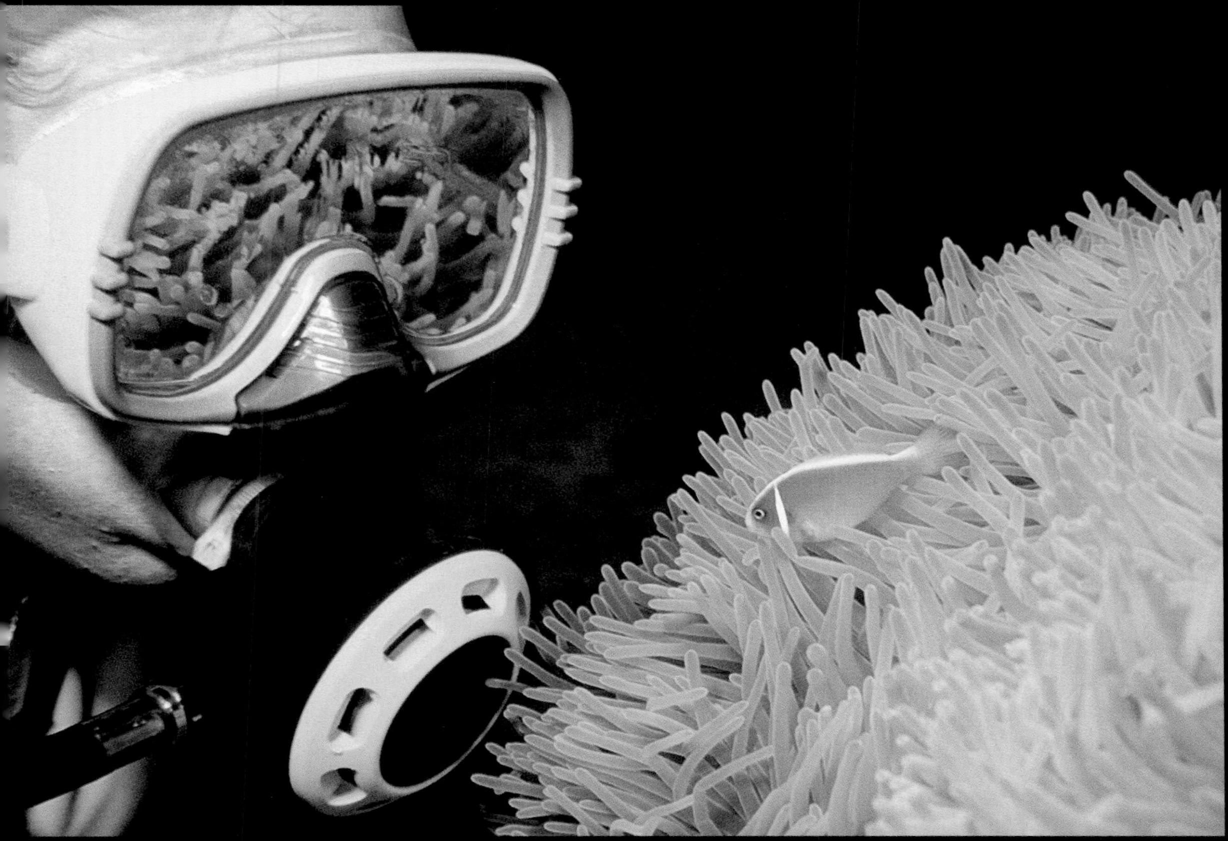

FISH THAT NORMALLY FEAR BOATS OR OTHER MAN-MADE STRUCTURES OFTEN SEEM TO WELCOME DIVERS SWIMMING AMONG THEM.

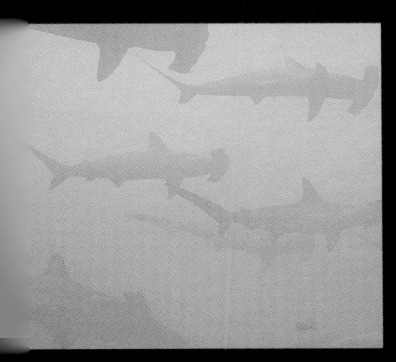

kelp *large seaweeds that grow in offshore beds in the temperate oceans; they are eaten in the Far East because of their high mineral and vitamin content*

ing and filming the underwater world, conducting scientific research, and refining scuba diving. They shared the beauty and mystery of a world filled with colorful **coral reefs**, giant **kelp** forests, and vast varieties of fish. They brought the world information about underwater fountains, craters, and caves.

One of the group's first expeditions was a risky one at the Fountain of Vaucluse in southern France. For centuries, no one knew why the Sorgue flooded at the same time each year. As Cousteau later explained, "A trickle flows from it the year around, until March comes; then the Fountain of Vaucluse erupts in a rage of water which swells the Sorgue

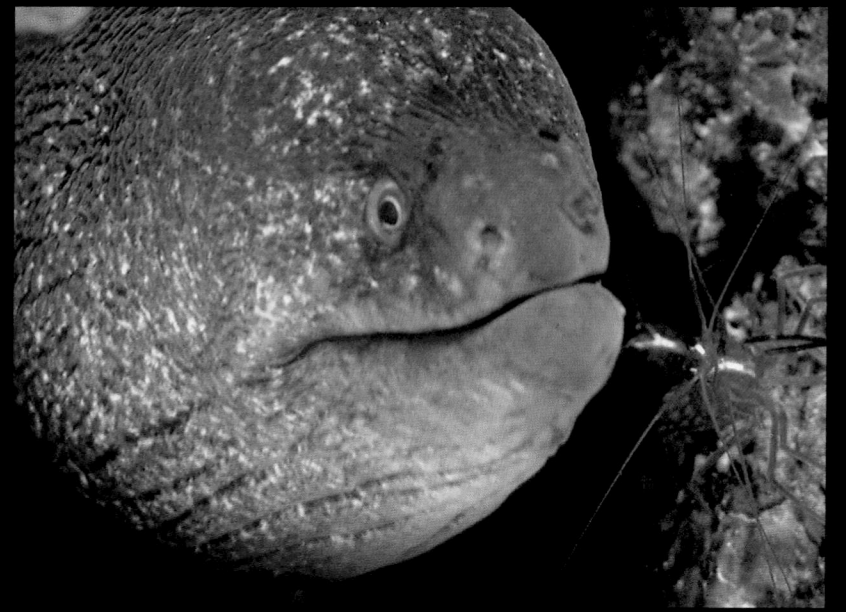

EELS, A KIND OF SNAKE-LIKE SEA CREATURE, OFTEN PEER AT SCUBA DIVERS FROM THE CREVICES OF UNDERWATER REEFS AND ROCK FORMATIONS.

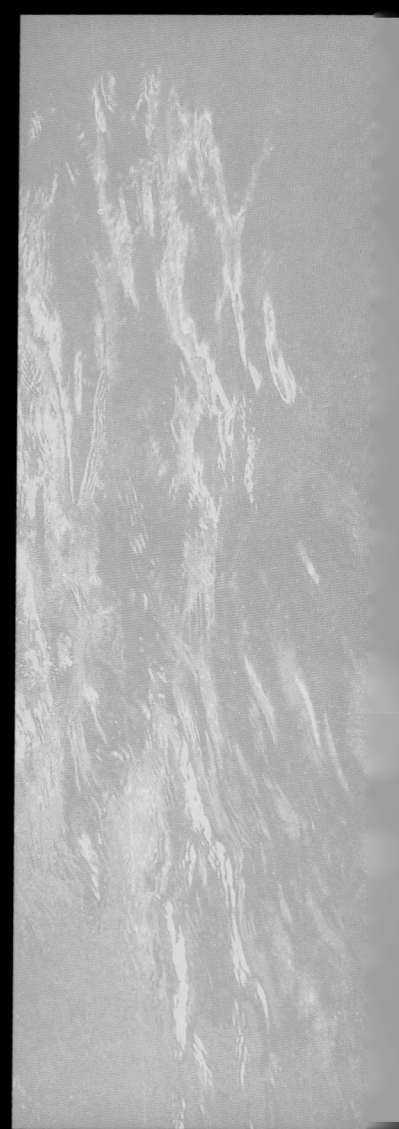

to flood. It pumps furiously for five weeks, then subsides." Cousteau and his friend Frédéric Dumas were nearly killed while exploring the deep cavern beneath a 200-foot (61 m) cliff.

In 1947, one member of Cousteau's group, Maurice Fargues, drowned in his attempt to set a new deep-water diving record. Cousteau vowed to commit to safety first in his underwater explorations. One of the safety measures he implemented was the use of a bathyscaphe (Greek for "deep boat") made by Swiss physicist Auguste Piccard. This underwater cylinder was built to withstand great pressure at depths down to 4,000 feet (1,219 m), allowing divers to explore deep realms without the dangers to the human body. Cousteau also devised an ingenious wet suit. A diver's body

In 1962, Jacques Cousteau began the Conshelf experiments. For one week, two "oceanauts" lived in a yellow cylinder 33 feet (10 m) underwater off the coast of Marseilles, France. Albert Falco and Claude Wesley would leave the habitat with scuba equipment to explore, but would return to the habitat to eat, sleep, and relax.

Whether a person is diving for recreation or research, the close interaction with the creatures of the sea is always thrilling.

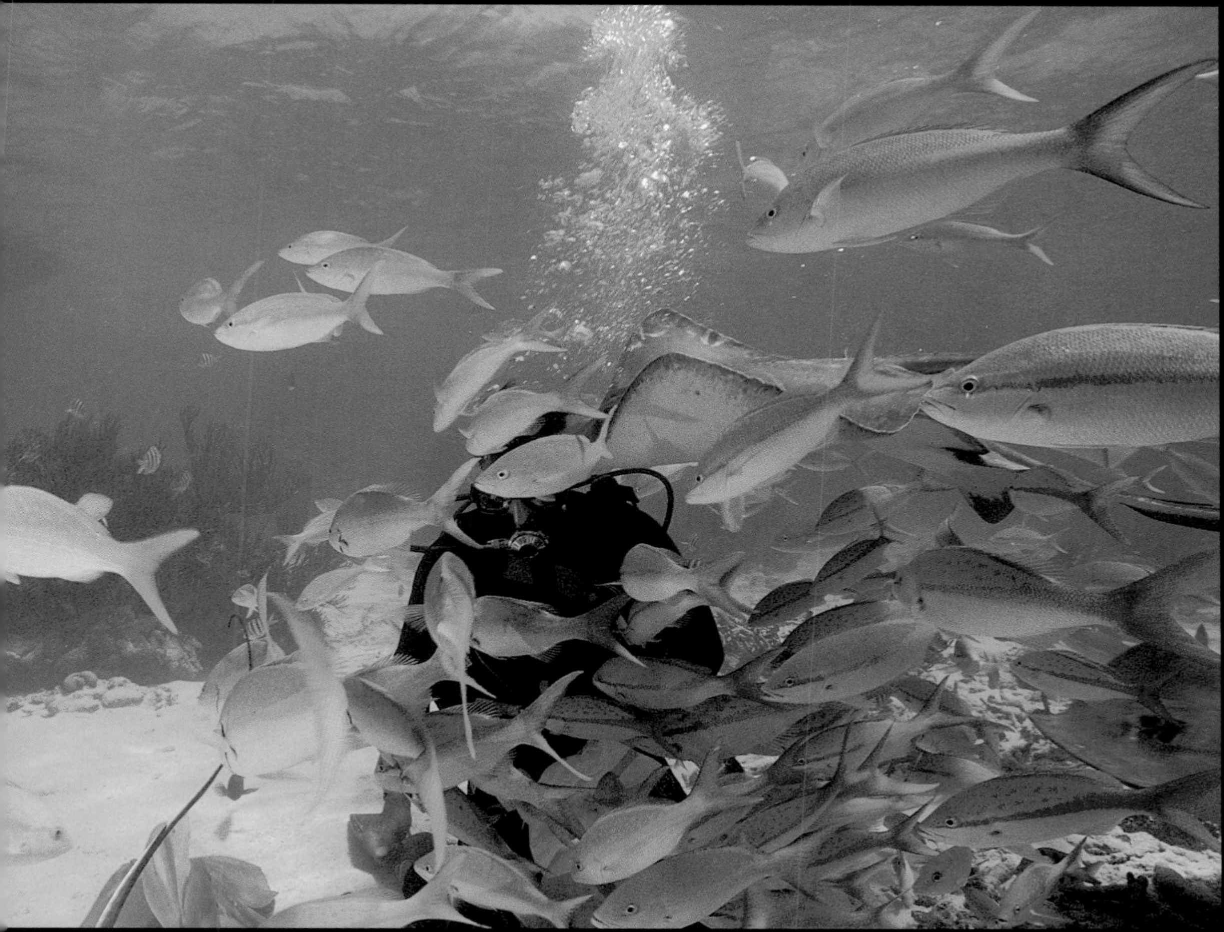

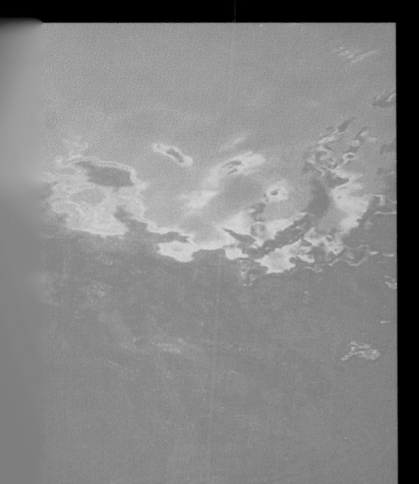

heat warmed a thin layer of water between the body and the suit, minimizing the effects of the extremely cold water at greater depths.

Many documentaries of the group's discoveries were shown on television. *Le Monde du Silence* (*The Silent World*), a film co-directed by Jacques Cousteau and Louis Malle, had its world premiere at the 1956 Cannes Film Festival, where the film won the festival's highest award. The following year, it won an Academy Award as the best documentary film. Cousteau continued diving until his death in 1997.

Dangers of the Deep

JACQUES COUSTEAU'S DIVERS experimented carefully with depth each time they entered the water. This cautious approach allowed them to warn others of a strange sensation that overcomes divers and can pose a threat to their lives: rapture of the deep.

In 1985, on Jacques Cousteau's 75th birthday, President Ronald Reagan presented Cousteau with America's highest civilian honor, the Medal of Freedom.

Scientifically known as nitrogen **narcosis**, rapture of the deep can affect a diver at various depths. Divers experience nitrogen narcosis when the increased water pressure at greater depths compresses the body's oxygen and allows the body to absorb more nitrogen. When too much nitrogen is absorbed by the body, narcosis occurs. At a depth of 100 feet (30.5 m), thinking and judgment are impaired, and fear can change to foolishness. Reality can turn into bizarre images, and dizziness can slip into sleep and then death.

Cousteau's close friend and diving partner, Frédéric "Didi" Dumas, lived to tell about his first experience with rapture of the deep. As he

swam deeper, he began to believe he was part man and part fish. He offered to share his air supply with a friendly fish that was passing by. Dizziness, then sleepiness, began to overtake him. Dumas was barely able to tie himself to the line going up to the boat. By the time he surfaced, the strange sensations were gone.

Divers must also avoid **decompression** sickness, an underwater disorder commonly known as "**the bends**." Gases are always dissolving in the human body, but the pressure at great depths increases the amount of gas in the body. If a diver ascends too quickly from a dive, the pressure is reduced too rapidly. The gases then form bubbles in the tissues or blood, causing a painful, serious condition. Divers can minimize the likelihood of the bends through careful planning and gradual ascent.

In the Antarctic summer of 1997–98, a team led by underwater photographer Norbert Wu took 68 scuba dives under the Antarctic ice to photograph sea life.

Other potential dangers in the sea include sharks and venomous sea snakes. The spines of sea urchins, or "porcupines

narcosis *unconsciousness produced by a chemical that dulls the senses*

decompression *a decrease in pressure, especially when a diver rises to the surface*

the bends *pain, breathing problems, and paralysis due to nitrogen bubbles forming in the blood when an underwater diver rises to the surface too fast*

hydroids *animals with stinging cells*

of the sea," can penetrate a diver's suit and break off in the flesh, inflicting a painful wound. **Hydroids** such as corals and jellyfish use nematocysts—stinging cells—to kill their food. The sting from the Portuguese man-of-war or the box jellyfish can send a person to the hospital.

Despite the many dangers posed by the aquatic environment, scuba diving is one of the safest outdoor sports. The potential for danger fosters a great respect for the underwater world among divers, who generally conduct themselves with a high degree of caution. Those who enter the underwater realm are well-trained and quickly learn to follow the self-imposed rules of the sport.

Certified to Dive

IT IS AN UNWRITTEN rule that equipment stores will not sell scuba gear or fill an air tank for anyone who does not have a diver's certification card. To become certified, a diver must enroll in a course approved by a certifying agency. Three of the major agencies are the National Association of Underwater Instructors, the Professional Association of Diving Instructors, and Scuba Schools International.

In 1952, Jacques Cousteau's divers discovered an old Roman freighter that had sunk in the Mediterranean Sea just south of France around 230 B.C. For an entire summer, Cousteau's team brought up thousands of wine jars, two-handled storage jugs, tiles, and coins.

Anyone over the age of 12 who has basic swimming skills can become a certified diver. Students receive approximately 30 hours of instruction that begins in a classroom, progresses to a swimming pool, and ends up in open water.

Instructors explain how each piece of equipment works and how water pressure affects divers. Understanding the effects of water pressure can save a diver's life. Although we cannot feel it, the air is constantly exerting one **atmosphere** of pressure on each square inch (6.5 sq cm) of our bodies. For every 33 feet (10 m) a diver descends underwater, there is

an extra atmosphere of pressure applied. Under the pressure of deep water, the air in a diver's lungs actually compresses. As the diver ascends, the air in the lungs expands. If a diver does not continue to breathe with a regular flow of air on the way to the surface, the air sacs in the lungs could burst, causing serious injury or death.

Students begin actual diving in a swimming pool. After passing a written exam and a pool exam, they dive several times in open water. These dives may take them as deep as 30 feet (9 m).

Certified scuba divers are ready to explore the underwater world with trusted friends. The foremost rule of safe diving is to never dive alone. Two divers often use a **buddy line** to keep track of each other. If a diver becomes stuck or if a reg-

atmosphere   *14.7 pounds (6.7 kg) of air pressure exerted on one square inch (6.5 sq cm) of the body; air pressure at sea level*

buddy line   *a rope connecting two divers*

ice diving   *diving in ice-covered waters; an ice diver enters and exits the water through a large hole cut in the ice*

A HUGE SCHOOL OF FISH SWIMS AHEAD OF A DIVER AND HIS CAMERA. THE COLORS FOUND BENEATH THE SEA CAN MAKE FOR SPECTACULAR PHOTOGRAPHS.

A SCUBA DIVER IN A RESEARCH CAGE GETS AN UP-CLOSE LOOK AT ONE OF THE MOST FEARED DANGERS OF THE DEEP—A GREAT WHITE SHARK.

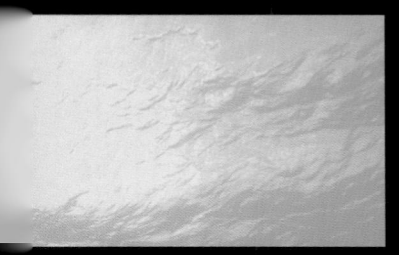

flight data recorders *also known as "black boxes," these instruments continually record information such as the altitude and speed of an aircraft*

submersibles *motor-powered underwater crafts used for research*

bathysphere *the first deep-sea craft, a steel sphere lowered from a ship by a cable*

ulator stops working, the other diver is always there to help.

Serious divers can also take advanced diving classes. They can learn the skills necessary for special endeavors such as night diving, underwater photography, **ice diving**, cave diving, and wreck diving. Divers need advanced training to qualify for certain underwater jobs, including working on telephone cables, pipelines, docks, and ships' hulls. Other divers' jobs include recovering **flight data recorders** and wreckage from aquatic airplane crashes. In the past, divers carried heavy equipment to underwater sites. Today, sophisticated **submersibles** transport equipment to aquatic work sites. Divers wear scuba equipment while operating these vehicles.

*On August 15, 1934, a **bathysphere** designed by William Beebe and Otis Barton made its deepest descent ever, traveling down 3,028 feet (923 m) off Bermuda.*

Diving for Adventure

OTHER DIVERS BESIDES Jacques Cousteau's groups have done extensive underwater research. Eugenie Clark is one diver who has combined her love for the aquatic world with a study of the creatures who live there. From the age of nine, Clark was fascinated with fish, especially sharks. On her first dive, she wore a heavy helmet and dive suit with air lines connected to a boat on the surface. After studying South Sea Islands fish for the United States government, Clark became the first director of the Cape Haze Marine Laboratory in Florida, where she studied sharks and other large fish in captivity. With the invention of scuba equipment, she began going to depths of 100 feet (30.5 m) or more to study sharks where they live.

In 1968, John Gruener and R. Neal Watson set a record by diving to 437 feet (133 m) off the coast of Grand Bahama Island, breathing compressed air. This record remained intact until 1990.

Clark's extensive work with sharks has earned her the title "Shark Lady" and a place among the most acclaimed divers of the century. "I want to keep on diving," Clark said. "I hope I will still be diving when I'm 90."

Another exciting aspect of scuba diving is exploring submerged history. Rich remnants of naval battles, luxury cruises, and ill-fated airplane flights are buried in the depths of the sea. Many diving clubs and resorts offer expeditions to see the dramatic remains of huge wrecks on the bottom of oceans or lakes. Of course, some ships and airplanes have come to rest at such great depths that only a submersible can transport people there. Those interested can rent or purchase small submarines for viewing wrecks at great depths.

The resting place of *Titanic*, the famous luxury liner that sank in 1912, remained a mystery until September 1, 1985. On that date, a group of explorers in a submersible found the once-mighty ship lying on the ocean floor at a depth of about 13,000 feet (3,962 m).

A DIVER STUDIES THE REMAINS OF THE *RHONE*, A MAIL BOAT THAT SANK NEAR THE BRITISH VIRGIN ISLANDS.

Wrecks provide a fascinating look at another time. An Italian luxury liner called the *Andrea Doria* was one of the largest and fastest ships of its era. It was also a kind of floating museum, carrying lavish murals, rare wood panels, ceramics, and mirrors designed by famous Italian artists. The ship sank in 1956 after colliding with a Swedish-American liner. In 1993, New Jersey diver John Moyer was awarded the exclusive right to bring up rare artifacts and art panels from the wreck.

Diver Art Cohn, the director of the Lake Champlain Maritime Museum,

Eugenie Clark discovered that the milky fluid of a fish called a Moses sole was poisonous and repulsive to sharks. It became a popular shark repellent for divers.

made an amazing discovery in the mid-1990s. At the bottom of Lake Champlain, a body of water between New York and Vermont, lay a 54-foot (16.5 m) vessel. Cohn recognized the wooden ship immediately. It was Benedict Arnold's gunboat, last used in 1776 during a Revolutionary War battle. The cold, deep water had preserved the vessel for 220 years.

Scuba diving can take people back in history, but it can also take us to new, unknown dimensions. Divers might encounter a coral reef, an unexplored cavern, or a life form unknown to human beings. Scuba divers are pioneers of a world that humans live with but seldom enter. Divers' adventures, photographs, and research help people to understand the vast waters of our planet—the strange and beautiful aquatic realm.

INDEX